United States Government Accountability Office

Report to the Committee
on Armed Services,
House of Representatives

I0410869

July 2014

NATIONAL NUCLEAR SECURITY ADMINISTRATION

Agency Expanded Use of Some Federal Oversight Reforms, but Is Still Determining Future Plans

GAO-14-588

GAO Highlights

Highlights of GAO-14-588, a report to the Committee on Armed Services, House of Representatives

NATIONAL NUCLEAR SECURITY ADMINISTRATION

Agency Expanded Use of Some Federal Oversight Reforms, but Is Still Determining Future Plans

Why GAO Did This Study

NNSA, a separately organized agency within DOE, has had long-standing problems managing its contracts and projects, which GAO has identified as being at high risk for fraud, waste, abuse, and mismanagement. Both DOE and, specifically, NNSA, undertook initiatives in 2002 and 2003 to improve contractor performance through revised federal oversight and greater contractor accountability. In 2006, concerned that efforts were moving too slowly, the NNSA Administrator tasked its KCP Field Office and contractor with implementing reforms at that site.

House Report 113-102, accompanying H.R. 1960, an early version of the National Defense Authorization Act for Fiscal Year 2014 mandated GAO to review the KCP reforms and issues with extending them to other NNSA sites. This report, among other things, (1) identifies key reforms implemented at KCP and reported benefits; (2) describes key factors NNSA and others identified as helping the site implement reforms; and (3) provides information on how NNSA has implemented and plans to implement similar reforms at other sites. GAO reviewed relevant documents prepared by NNSA, DOE, contractors, and others; visited KCP; and discussed the reforms with cognizant federal officials and contractor staff.

During GAO's review, Congress required NNSA to develop a study and plan for implementing the principles of the Kansas City reforms at its other sites. In light of the congressional requirement, GAO is not making additional recommendations at this time. NNSA generally agreed with the findings of this report.

View GAO-14-588. For more information, contact David C. Trimble at (202) 512-3841 or trimbled@gao.gov.

What GAO Found

Key reforms at the National Nuclear Security Administration's (NNSA) Kansas City Plant (KCP)—a site in Missouri that manufactures electronic and other nonnuclear components of nuclear weapons—included (1) streamlining operating requirements by replacing Department of Energy (DOE) requirements with industry standards, where appropriate; (2) refocusing federal oversight to rely on contractor performance data for lower-risk activities; and (3) establishing clear contractor goals and incentives. A 2008 review of the reforms reported nearly $14 million in cost reductions were achieved at the site by implementing these reforms.

NNSA and KCP federal and contractor staff identified key factors that facilitated implementation of reforms at KCP, including the following:

- **High-level support from NNSA and field office leadership**. Gaining and maintaining the support of the NNSA Administrator and buy-in of some KCP Field Office staff for changes from the reforms was critical.
- **Unique site conditions and operations**. Conditions at KCP enabled implementation of the proposed reforms, including (1) the comparability of the site's activities and operations to those of commercial industry; (2) the site's relatively low-risk, nonnuclear activities generally did not involve or potentially affect nuclear safety and security; and (3) the site was managed by a contractor owned by a single corporate parent with a reputation for quality.
- **A cooperative federal-contractor partnership**. A cooperative relationship between the KCP Field Office and the contractor facilitated implementation of the reforms.

NNSA has extended to other sites some elements of the reforms, including (1) encouraging greater use of industry standards, where appropriate; (2) directing field office oversight staff to rely more on contractor self-assessment of performance for lower-risk activities; and (3) setting clearer contractor goals by revising how the agency evaluates annual contractor performance. However, NNSA and DOE are re-evaluating implementation of some of these reforms after a July 2012 security breach at an NNSA site, where overreliance on contractor self-assessments was identified by reviews of the event as a contributing factor. Moreover, NNSA officials and other studies noted that key factors enabling implementation of reforms at KCP may not exist at NNSA's other sites. For example, most NNSA sites conduct high-hazard activities, which may involve nuclear materials and require higher safety and security standards than KCP. NNSA is evaluating further implementation of such reforms and expects to report to Congress its findings later in 2014.

Contents

Abbreviations

DOE	Department of Energy
HSS	Office of Health, Safety, and Security
ISO	International Standards Organization
KCP	Kansas City Plant
LLC	limited liability company
M&O	management and operating
NAP	NNSA Policy Letter
NNSA	National Nuclear Security Administration
Science	Office of Science

July 17, 2014

The Honorable Howard P. "Buck" McKeon
Chairman
The Honorable Adam Smith
Ranking Member
Committee on Armed Services
House of Representatives

The National Nuclear Security Administration (NNSA), a separately organized agency within the Department of Energy (DOE), is responsible for managing nuclear weapon- and nonproliferation-related missions in research and development laboratories, production plants, and other facilities—known collectively as the nuclear security enterprise.[1] NNSA directs these national security missions, but work activities are largely carried out by contractors under management and operating (M&O) contracts at NNSA's eight government-owned, contractor-operated sites.[2] To implement its programs, NNSA relies on M&O contractors to manage day-to-day site operations and to adhere to laws and regulations and requirements provided in DOE and NNSA directives[3] when operating the laboratories, production plants, and other sites within the complex.

---

[1] Specifically, NNSA manages three national nuclear weapon design laboratories—Lawrence Livermore National Laboratory in California, Los Alamos National Laboratory in New Mexico, and Sandia National Laboratories in New Mexico and California; three nuclear weapons production sites—the Kansas City Plant in Missouri, the Pantex Plant in Texas, and the Y-12 National Security Complex in Tennessee; and the Nevada National Security Site, formerly known as the Nevada Test Site. NNSA also manages the Tritium Facilities at DOE's Savannah River Site in South Carolina.

[2] M&O contracts are agreements under which the government contracts for the operation, maintenance, or support, on its behalf, of a government-owned or –controlled research, development, special production, or testing establishment wholly or principally devoted to one or more of the major programs of the contracting agency. The M&O contractors generally carry out the mission and activities of the particular contract on a daily basis, while following federal laws and regulations, and applicable requirements from DOE policies, orders, and guides and manuals, known as directives.

[3] The department's system of directives includes policies, orders, and guides and manuals. These directives may contain mandatory requirements, as well as nonmandatory guidance for implementing requirements. For purposes of this report, we refer to all these components as directives. In addition to DOE directives, NNSA has issued directives specific to its sites. These directives are generally referred to as NNSA Policy Letters, or NAPs.

Because many NNSA sites conduct hazardous operations and handle special nuclear material that can be used in nuclear weapons, such as plutonium-239 or highly enriched uranium,[4] effective federal oversight is critical to ensuring that national security, human health and safety, and the environment are not harmed.

Long-standing problems have led us to designate DOE's and, subsequently, NNSA's contract and project management as high risk for fraud, waste, abuse, and mismanagement since 1990—the first year we published the high-risk list.[5] To address these problems, both the department and, specifically, NNSA, have undertaken initiatives to improve contractor performance through revised federal oversight and greater contractor accountability. In April 2002, for example, the DOE Undersecretary outlined approaches for improving Office of Science[6] contract performance and promoting greater contractor accountability by, among other things, (1) relying primarily on federal, state, and local laws, regulations, and national standards, while minimizing the use of DOE directives; (2) using third-party certification by nationally recognized experts to supplement federal oversight and to certify that the contractor's management systems meet applicable laws and regulations; and, (3) moving from an oversight approach of compliance against requirements to reviewing a contractor's system for identifying and correcting problems. In December 2002, NNSA announced a similar initiative to improve and

---

[4]Uranium is categorized by concentration of uranium-235, expressed as a percentage "assay." Natural uranium has an assay of about 0.7 percent uranium-235. For use in a nuclear reactor or weapon, natural uranium must be enriched to increase its assay to a level required for its ultimate use. For example, low enriched uranium, which is used in commercial nuclear power reactors, typically has an assay of between 3 and 5 percent uranium-235. Highly enriched uranium is used in nuclear weapons.

[5]GAO, *Government Financial Vulnerability: 14 Areas Needing Special Review*, GAO/OCG-90-1 (Washington, D.C.: Jan. 23, 1990). In 2013, we shifted our focus concerning the high-risk area to DOE's Office of Environmental Management and NNSA major projects (i.e., those with values of at least $750 million) to acknowledge progress made in managing smaller- value efforts. GAO, *High-Risk Series: An Update*, GAO-13-283 (Washington, D.C.: February 2013).

[6]With a $4.9 billion budget in fiscal year 2011—18 percent of DOE's total budget—the Office of Science (Science) has been the nation's single largest funding source for basic research in the physical sciences, supporting research in energy sciences, advanced scientific computing, and other fields. Science funds research at DOE's 10 national laboratories, which also house scientific facilities and equipment, ranging from high-performance computers to ultrabright X-ray sources for investigating fundamental properties of materials.

GAO-14-588 Extension of Kansas City Reforms

streamline federal oversight of its M&O contractors by reviewing the M&O contractor's assurance systems, processes, and data instead of monitoring certain lower-risk activities, such as business operations. Under this approach, contractors would self-monitor lower-risk activities. In 2003, the Secretary of Energy tasked other offices within the department with implementing similar reforms to those of the Office of Science and NNSA across the department. In April 2006, concerned that efforts to improve contractor performance were moving too slowly, the NNSA Administrator tasked NNSA's Kansas City Plant (KCP)[7]—a site that manufactures electronic and other nonnuclear components for nuclear weapons—with implementing management and oversight reforms.

The 2006 KCP reforms consisted of a set of actions to improve contractor performance, accountability, and efficiency, which, according to KCP Field Office (the collocated federally staffed office that oversees KCP operations) [8] officials at the time, could lead to cost savings. Reforms included revising M&O contract provisions to incorporate, where appropriate, industry standards in place of DOE requirements and reduced direct NNSA oversight of some contractor activities deemed to be of lower risk, such as business operations, relying instead on the contractor's own oversight system to catch and correct problems on lower risk activities. Some aspects of the KCP reforms have been implemented at other NNSA sites. According to DOE's Office of Inspector General, reforms similar to those implemented at KCP may have contributed to a July 2012 security breach at the Y-12 National Security Complex in

---

[7] In this report, "KCP" refers to the NNSA site, including both its M&O contractor and the collocated federal NNSA field office.

[8] This office was formerly known as the Kansas City Site Office during the reform implementation period.

Tennessee, whose root causes are similar to some of the reforms implemented at KCP.[9]

House Report 113-102, accompanying H.R. 1960, an early version of the National Defense Authorization Act for Fiscal Year 2014,[10] mandated GAO to review the KCP reforms and issues related to extending these reforms to other NNSA sites. Accordingly, this report (1) identifies the key reforms implemented at KCP and reported benefits; (2) describes the key factors that NNSA, KCP and others identified as helping the site implement reforms; and (3) provides information on how NNSA has implemented or plans to implement similar reforms at other sites. We provided an oral briefing of our preliminary results to your staff on November 15, 2013. Subsequent to our briefing, section 3130 of the National Defense Authorization Act for Fiscal Year 2014 was enacted and requires the NNSA Administrator to develop a feasibility study and plan that, among other things, examines the applicability of all or some of the principles of the KCP reforms to additional facilities in the national security enterprise by June 2014.

To describe the KCP reforms, reported benefits, as well as key factors that NNSA and KCP officials identified as helping the site develop and implement reforms, we reviewed NNSA, DOE, and contractor documents relating to the development and implementation of the KCP reforms. We also visited KCP and discussed the reforms, the implementation process, and current status with federal and contractor officials. We also reviewed assessments of the KCP reforms. We analyzed NNSA cost-reduction estimates resulting from implementing the reforms and discussed these with KCP Field Office officials and contractor representatives at KCP. In

---

[9]During the security breach at the Y-12 National Security Complex, three trespassers gained access to the protected security area directly adjacent to one of the nation's most critically important nuclear weapon–related facilities without being interrupted by the security measures in place. According to DOE's Inspector General, this security incident was unprecedented and represented multiple system failures including failures to maintain critical security equipment, respond properly to alarms, and understand security protocols. The Inspector General found that contractor governance and federal oversight did not identify and correct early indications of these multiple system breakdowns. U.S. Department of Energy, Office of Inspector General, Office of Audits and Inspections, *Special Report: Inquiry Into the Security Breach at the National Nuclear Security Administration's Y-12 National Security Complex*, DOE/IG-0868 (Washington, D.C.: Aug. 29, 2012).

[10]The bill ultimately enacted into law as the National Defense Authorization Act for Fiscal Year 2014, Pub. L. No. 113-66, 127 Stat. 672, was H.R. 3304.

addition, we discussed cost-reduction estimates with the author of a January 2008 study commissioned by the KCP contractor to assess the cost reductions associated with the reforms and the degree to which the reforms were implemented. To obtain information on the extent to which NNSA has implemented or plans to implement KCP reforms at other sites, we discussed the reforms with NNSA's Associate Principal Deputy Administrator. We also discussed the reforms with independent experts, including officials from DOE's Office of Health, Safety, and Security; the Defense Nuclear Facilities Safety Board;[11] the National Academy of Public Administration; the National Academy of Sciences; and a representative from J.W. Bibler & Associates, contracted by the KCP contractor to assess cost reductions associated with implementation of the reforms.

We conducted this performance audit from July 2013 to July 2014 in accordance with generally accepted government auditing standards. Those standards require that we plan and perform the audit to obtain sufficient, appropriate evidence to provide a reasonable basis for our findings and conclusions based on our audit objectives. We believe that the evidence obtained provides a reasonable basis for our findings and conclusions based on our audit objectives.

Background

To carry out NNSA's nuclear weapons and nonproliferation missions, contractors at the eight NNSA sites conduct research, manufacturing, testing at facilities located at those sites. (See fig. 1.)

[11]The Defense Nuclear Facilities Safety Board is an independent executive branch agency created to independently assess safety conditions and operations at defense nuclear facilities at DOE and NNSA sites.

Figure 1: National Nuclear Security Administration (NNSA) Research, Production, and Testing Sites

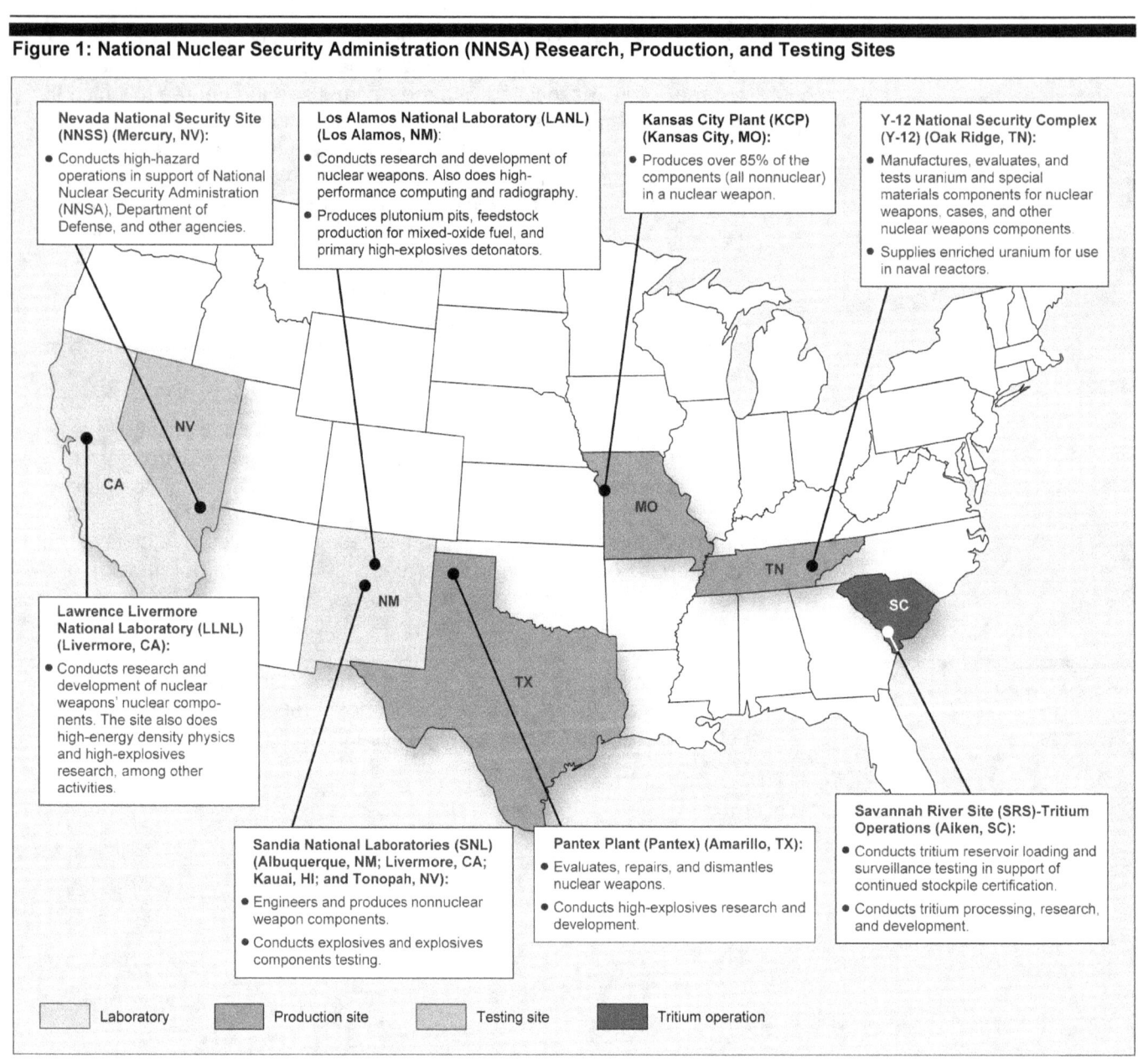

Sources: National Nuclear Security Administration; Map Resources (map). | GAO-14-588

DOE establishes safety or security requirements based on a categorization of site-specific risks, including hazardous operations and the presence of special nuclear material—material which can be used in producing nuclear weapons. Federal regulations define three categories of nuclear facilities based on the potential significance of radiological consequences in the event of a nuclear accident. These categories range from Hazard category 1 nuclear facilities with the potential for off-site radiological consequences, to Hazard category 2 nuclear facilities with the potential for significant on-site radiological consequences beyond the facility but which would be contained within the site, to Hazard category 3 nuclear facilities with the potential for significant radiological consequences at only the immediate area of the facility. In terms of security, DOE's security orders establish levels of security protection according to a site's types and quantities of special nuclear material. Special nuclear material is classified according to 4 levels—Category I (highest risk) to Category IV (lowest risk).[12] Accordingly, DOE's sites with Category I nuclear materials—including specified quantities and forms of special nuclear material such as nuclear weapons and nuclear weapons components—require the highest level of security since the risks may include the theft of a nuclear weapon or creation of an improvised nuclear device capable of producing a nuclear explosion.

As discussed earlier, work activities to support NNSA's national security missions are largely carried out by M&O contractors. This arrangement has historical roots. Since the Manhattan Project produced the first atomic bomb during World War II, DOE, NNSA, and predecessor agencies have depended on the expertise of private firms, universities, and others to carry out research and development work and operate the facilities necessary for the nation's nuclear defense. Currently, DOE spends 90 percent of its annual budget on M&O contracts, making it the largest non-Department of Defense contracting agency in the government. NNSA's M&O contractors are largely limited liability companies consisting of

---

[12]Regarding security, DOE's security policies establish levels of security protection required according to a site's quantities and types of special nuclear material. As defined in DOE security policy, lesser quantities of special nuclear material —Category II, III, and IV quantities—are not, by themselves, capable of producing a nuclear yield but must be secured to prevent theft for use in radioactive dispersal or to accumulate Category I quantities. Four of NNSA's sites have facilities that process and store Category I special nuclear material, which receives the highest levels of security protection. These four sites are the Y-12 National Security Complex in Oak Ridge, TN; Pantex Plant in Amarillo, TX; Los Alamos National Laboratory in Los Alamos, NM, and the National Nuclear Security Site in Mercury, NV. KCP is considered a Category IV—the lowest risk—site.

multiple member companies.[13] Contractors at only two NNSA sites—the KCP and Sandia National Laboratories—are owned by a sole parent corporation.[14]

NNSA requires its contractors to adhere to federal laws, departmental regulations, and DOE and NNSA requirements that are provided in the department's system of directives, including policies, orders, guides, and manuals. The agency incorporates directives into contracts and holds contractors accountable for meeting the associated requirements. Contractors, NNSA, DOE, and other organizations manage and oversee operations through a multitiered approach. First, contractors manage operations, conduct self-assessments, and perform corrective actions to maintain compliance with government expectations. Second, NNSA headquarters organizations (1) set processes and corporate expectations for contractors managing the sites, (2) have primary responsibility for ensuring contractors are performing and adhering to contract requirements, and (3) evaluate contractor performance. Third, NNSA's field offices oversee the contractors on a daily basis. This includes on-site monitoring and evaluating contractor work activities. Fourth, entities outside of NNSA provide independent oversight of contractor performance. In particular, DOE's Office of Health, Safety, and Security (HSS),[15] is responsible for, among other things, developing the department's safety and security policy, providing independent oversight of contractor compliance with DOE's safety and security regulations and directives, and conducting enforcement activities. The Defense Nuclear Facilities Safety Board also provides oversight of nuclear safety that is independent of NNSA and DOE.

---

[13]A limited liability company (LLC) is an entity that blends elements of partnerships—such as management by members and limitations on ownership transfer—and corporations—such as limited liability.

[14]KCP is operated by Honeywell Federal Manufacturing & Technologies, LLC, a wholly owned subsidiary of the Honeywell Corporation—a Fortune 100 company. Sandia National Laboratories is operated by the Sandia Corporation, a wholly owned subsidiary of the Lockheed Martin Corporation, which is also a Fortune 100 company.

[15] Under a recent departmental reorganization, this office is now called the Office of Independent Enterprise Assessments. In this report, we refer to the office as the Office of Health, Safety, and Security.

According to NNSA and KCP Officials, KCP Reforms to Streamline Requirements, Refocus Federal Oversight, and Establish Clear Contractor Incentives Produced a Number of Benefits

In implementing its new management and oversight approach in 2007, KCP implemented reforms that sought to (1) streamline operating requirements, (2) refocus federal oversight, and (3) provide clear contractor goals and meaningful incentives. KCP reported that these actions produced a number of benefits, including cost reductions at the site. According to the KCP Field Office and contractor, KCP under took the following actions:

- **Streamlined operating requirements.** The KCP Field Office sought to streamline operating requirements and limit the imposition of new DOE requirements in the future. These changes included eliminating, where possible, some DOE directives and replacing others with industry or site-specific standards, such as quality assurance requirements and emergency management requirements. The contractor remained obligated to meet all applicable federal laws and regulations. According to the contractor, by 2009, the site had reduced 160 operating requirements from specific DOE orders, regulations, and other standards to 71 site operating requirements. For example, the site replaced requirements from DOE's quality assurance order[16] with quality assurance processes outlined in the International Standards Organization's Standard 9001-2008,[17] an international standard used in private industry to ensure that quality and continuous improvement are built into all work processes. KCP was also able to eliminate its on-site fire department by relying on municipal firefighting services to fulfill a DOE requirement for site fire protection capability.[18] To help limit future growth of requirements, KCP implemented a directives change control board. This group, with

---

[16]DOE defines quality as an item, service, or process that meets or exceeds the user's requirements and expectations. See DOE Order 414.1D, *Quality Assurance* (Washington, D.C.: Apr. 24, 2011).

[17]The International Standards Organization (ISO), an independent, nongovernmental organization made up of the members of the national standards bodies from 164 countries, develops voluntary standards to help promote a consistent set of specifications for products, services, and best practices to promote efficient international trade.

[18] DOE nuclear and worker safety directives require sites to establish fire protection programs that include emergency response and access to fire protection staff. See DOE Order 420.1C, *Facility Safety* (Washington, D.C.: Dec. 4, 2012); DOE Order 151.1C, *Comprehensive Emergency Management System* (Washington, D.C.: Nov. 2, 2005); and DOE Order 440.1B, *Worker Protection Program for DOE (Including the National Nuclear Security Administration) Federal Employees* (Washington, D.C.: Aug. 21, 2012). KCP reported a more than $465,000 cost reduction in fiscal years 2008 and 2009 by eliminating its on-site fire department.

joint federal Field Office and contractor staff membership, reviews new or revised directives to determine their applicability to the contract, rejecting those requirements not deemed to be relevant. According to a KCP Field Office official, since 2007, the board has rejected 235 of 370 new directives issued by DOE and other sources.[19] The KCP Field Office official noted that reasons for rejecting directives include their inapplicability to a nonnuclear site or because the new directive requirements were already covered in KCP's site-specific standards.

- **Refocused federal oversight**. The KCP Field Office sought to refocus federal oversight by (1) changing its approach from reviewing compliance with requirements to monitoring contractor assurance systems for lower-risk activities; (2) exerting greater control over audit findings at the field office level; and (3) increasing its use of external reviewers. First, the field office changed its oversight approach from reviewing compliance of all contractor activities to allowing the contractor to assume responsibility for ensuring performance in lower-risk activities, allowing federal staff to concentrate resources on monitoring high-risk activities such as safety and security. In this approach, the field office moved from a traditional "transactional" oversight—in which performance is determined by federal oversight staff checking compliance against requirements—to a "systems-based" oversight—in which performance on lower-risk activities is ensured by monitoring the contractor's systems, processes, and data, including its systems of self-assessment and actions to correct problems. According to KCP Field Office officials, federal oversight staff assumed the role of reviewing the contractor's management and oversight systems, as well as reviewing selected data provided by these systems, to ensure adequate processes were in place to identify and correct problems.

Second, the field office exerted greater control over audit findings from external reviews, by determining which findings would need to be addressed by the contractor.[20] According to KCP Field Office and

---

[19] According to a KCP Field Office official, the 370 directives include new and updated DOE orders, manuals, guides, supplemental directives, and other sources that are used to establish requirements.

[20] Contractors are generally required to develop corrective actions in response to audit findings that will address the cause of the findings and prevent recurrence. DOE, *Implementation of Department of Energy Oversight Policy*, DOE Order 226.1B (Washington, D.C.: Apr. 25, 2011).

GAO-14-588 Extension of Kansas City Reforms

contractor officials, this ability to accept or reject audit findings from external reviews enabled the field office to prevent implementation of new requirements that would not be applicable at the site. According to another KCP Field Office official, although the field office had this authority under the reforms, it had not rejected any audit findings. Finally, to revise its oversight approach, the KCP Field Office relied more on third-party assessments or certifications of contractor performance in place of federal oversight reviews, according to a field office official. Such assessments included those by the contractor's parent corporation, as well as external groups, such as the Excellence in Missouri Foundation, which administers the Missouri Quality Award to promote quality in business in the state.

- **Clear contractor goals and meaningful incentives.** KCP Field Office officials noted that, under the reforms, the Field Office and the contractor agreed on five outcome areas for contractor performance, and performance award fees were linked to these outcome areas. This differed from the previous approach under which performance award fees were linked to meeting headquarters expectations and directive requirements. KCP Field Office officials noted this allowed them to focus performance award fee on "what" a contractor does, rather than on "how" it meets requirements. Under the reforms, the five outcome areas on which performance would be evaluated included: (1) meeting product schedule; (2) meeting product specification; (3) managing cost; (4) managing assets and resources, including facilities, inventory, and staff; and (5) meeting contract standards. Under the reforms, each year, the KCP Field Office highlighted performance areas of major importance to encourage the contractor to focus resources on those areas, rather than expending resources on what the field office and contractor agrees are less important goals and requirements. In this framework, the contractor is eligible to earn the majority of associated fees as long as adequate performance was achieved. According to the KCP Field Office implementing plan, this differed from the previous approach, under which the contractor needed to exceed performance expectations to earn more than 60 percent of an award fee. KCP Field Office officials noted a key to effective contract management under the reforms was the ability of the field office to hold the contractor accountable by focusing fee on desired outcomes.

In implementing the reforms, the site reported it was able to reduce costs in its initial year of implementation, some of which was achieved by decreasing oversight staff. A January 2008 review commissioned by the KCP Field Office to assess cost savings resulting from implementing the reforms[21] reported the Field Office achieved a cost reduction of $936,000 in fiscal year 2007 by eliminating, through attrition, eight full-time staff positions. The total savings this review reported was nearly $14 million (fiscal year 2006 dollars) which comprised cost reductions that had been achieved in fiscal 2007 directly or indirectly by implementing the KCP reforms. This reported $14 million in cost reductions was about 3 percent of the site's overall fiscal year 2007 budget of about $434 million. According to a KCP Field Office official, no further analyses of cost savings has been conducted since that time.

NNSA and KCP Identified Key Factors As Helping Reform Implementation

Reviews of the reforms, as well as NNSA and KCP Field Office and contractor officials, cited several important factors that assisted with implementation of the reforms at the site. Key factors included having (1) high-level support from leadership for reforms, (2) site specific conditions and operations, and (3) a cooperative federal-contractor partnership.

- **High-level support from NNSA and field office leadership and key stakeholders.** According to a 2008 KCP Field Office review of lessons learned from implementing the reforms, gaining and maintaining the support of the NNSA Administrator and buy-in from some of the KCP federal staff for changes was critical to their implementation.[22] With the support of the NNSA Administrator, the KCP Field Office Manager was given clear authority and responsibility to make the changes necessary to implement the reforms. According to the 2008 review, implementation required getting support from federal staff at the site, whose oversight activities were likely to change because of the reforms. The KCP Field Office Assistant Manager told us field office staff involved in oversight at the site were initially reluctant to make the necessary changes to their oversight activities—such as moving away from a compliance-type oversight approach to relying on reviews of contractor assurance systems—but

---

[21]J.W. Bibler & Associates, *Kansas City Site Office Oversight Plan: Assessment of Implementation Cost Savings*, under Kansas City Plant Purchase Order 224832 (January 2008).

[22]U.S. Department of Energy, National Nuclear Security Administration, *Lessons Learned Report: Implementation of the Kansas City Plant Site Office Oversight Plan at the Kansas City Plant* (Washington, D.C.: April 2008).

they ultimately agreed to the changes. The 2008 KCP Field Office review of lessons learned noted that acceptance by stakeholders was more easily obtained for reforms such as applying industry standards because of the unique operations at KCP, which included lower risk, nonnuclear activities. These stakeholders included program offices within NNSA. Other stakeholders were more qualified in their support. For example, DOE's HSS reported in a March 2008 review of the KCP reforms that, overall, the reform framework had the potential for providing sufficient federal oversight at reduced cost for the site.[23] The report also found, however, that some weaknesses existed in implementing the reforms, such as the field office not being able to complete a significant percentage of scheduled security oversight reviews and observations in fiscal year 2007 due to staffing shortages and not having adequate reviews of site-specific standards for safeguards and security.

- **Unique site conditions and operations.** In selecting KCP to implement the reforms in 2006, the NNSA Administrator noted that, in comparison to NNSA's other sites, unique conditions existed at the site that enabled implementation of the proposed reforms. These conditions included (1) KCP operations, which are largely manufacturing, were comparable to those of commercial industry, most notably the aerospace industry; (2) activities at the site were largely lower-risk, nonnuclear, and generally did not involve or potentially affect nuclear safety and security; and (3) the site contractor was owned by a single corporate parent—Honeywell—that has, according to a Field Office official, well-developed corporate management systems and a commitment to quality. In addition, the implementation of reforms at KCP was undertaken at a time of broader operational changes at KCP. More specifically, NNSA was in the process of modernizing KCP operations to lower operations and maintenance costs. This included building and relocating to a new modernized production facility and increasing the use of external suppliers for nonnuclear components rather than producing the components in-house. According to a KCP Field Office official, as of

---

[23]U.S. Department of Energy, Office of Health, Safety and Security, Office of Independent Oversight; *Independent Oversight Special Review of the Kansas City Plant Site Office Plan for Line Oversight* (Washington, D.C.: March 2008).

April 2014, more than 70 percent of operations had been moved to the new facility.[24]

- **A cooperative federal-contractor partnership.** The KCP Field Office noted in its April 2008 review of lessons learned from implementing the reforms that development of the reforms was enabled because of a cooperative relationship between the field office and the contractor. According to the review, a steering committee with members from both the KCP Field Office and the contractor managed the implementation of the reforms. These members agreed to the overall objectives and key elements of the reforms early in the process and worked together to develop those key reforms. According to this field office review, this cooperative relationship not only eased implementation of the reforms but assisted in gaining approval for the reforms from NNSA and DOE headquarters officials. The January 2008 study assessing cost reductions resulting from implementing the reforms found that this cooperation between site federal and contractor officials had developed over a period of years.[25]

In addition, KCP Field Office officials told us that having the leadership and involvement by the contractor's parent corporation resulted in greater accountability. According to a 2009 review commissioned by NNSA to assess the reforms,[26] the parent corporation was responsible for setting core processes and policies, determining best practices to be implemented, and ensuring the field office maintained transparency in how the site was managed. This was a change from the previous approach, whereby the contractor adhered to NNSA-set expectations and requirements. In addition, under the reforms, the contractor was allowed to leverage corporate management systems, in place of DOE-required systems to manage work and performance. KCP Field Office officials noted that, although

---

[24]We examined the costs associated with Kansas City Plant's new facility in GAO, *Nuclear Weapons: National Nuclear Security Administration Needs to Better Manage Risks Associated with Modernization of Its Kansas City Plant*, GAO-10-115 (Washington: D.C.: Oct. 23, 2009).

[25]In 1949 the Atomic Energy Commission—a predecessor to the Department of Energy—asked the Bendix Corporation to build the nonnuclear components of nuclear bombs at the KCP. Bendix merged with Allied Corporation in 1983, which went on to merge with Honeywell in 1999.

[26]Engineered Resources, LLC, *The KCP Oversight Model: What It Is — and Isn't*, prepared under Department of Energy contract No.DE-AC04-01AL66850 (Augusta, GA: Nov. 16, 2009).

the contractor was held responsible for the agreed-upon mission performance outcomes, it fell to both the contractor and the parent company to fix any problems. According to the 2009 review, allowing the contractor to use corporate management systems resulted in encouraging the parent company to take a more active part in providing oversight.

NNSA Has Implemented Some KCP-Like Reforms at Its Other Sites, but Applicability and Future Plans Are Still Being Determined

Since the 2007 implementation of reforms at KCP, NNSA has taken steps to extend some elements of the site's reforms at other NNSA sites and to integrate the reforms into subsequent agency-wide initiatives to improve contractor performance and accountability. However, NNSA is revisiting the reforms following a July 2012 security breach at one of its sites, and NNSA's future plans to continue extending KCP-like reforms at its other sites are currently uncertain.

After KCP undertook implementation of its reforms in 2007, NNSA began to implement similar reforms at selected sites and subsequently, incorporated elements of the reforms into agency-wide initiatives to improve oversight and management of M&O contractors. At the site level, in 2009, the NNSA Administrator formed an internal team to look at ways of accelerating efforts to implement KCP-like reforms at other NNSA sites, where appropriate. In addition, in February 2010, the NNSA Administrator tasked officials at the Sandia National Laboratories and Nevada Test Site with implementing reforms similar to those implemented at KCP for nonnuclear activities. These two sites were to, among other things, (1) streamline operating requirements by identifying opportunities to eliminate some agency requirements and make greater use of industry standards; (2) refocus federal oversight by, among other things, making greater use of the contractor's management system; and (3) set clear contractor goals and meaningful incentives following the KCP approach. The two sites were tasked with identifying cost efficiencies associated with implementing these reforms.

In 2010, NNSA issued two Policy Letters that sought to streamline security requirements for the control of classified information, such as classified documents and electronic media, and on the physical protection of facilities, property, personnel, and national security interests, such as special nuclear material. These two policy letters were included in NNSA's M&O contracts in place of the corresponding DOE directives.

Subsequently, in 2011, NNSA issued a new policy for all of its sites that outlined basic requirements for a new oversight and management approach that had roots in the KCP reforms.[27] This new policy—called "transformational governance"—directed, for example, site oversight staff to focus greater efforts on assessing contractor performance in higher-risk activities, such as security, and for lower-risk activities, rely more heavily on monitoring contractor assurance systems. More broadly, DOE was undertaking similar reforms during this period. Specifically, in March 2010, the Deputy Secretary of Energy announced an initiative to revise DOE's safety and security directives by streamlining or eliminating duplicative requirements, revising federal oversight and encouraging greater use of industry standards. As we reported in 2012, DOE's effort resulted in reducing the overall number of directives. For example, DOE reduced its number of safety directives from 80 to 42.[28]

However, according to NNSA officials, since the July 2012 security breach at NNSA's Y-12 National Security Complex in Oak Ridge, Tennessee, some of NNSA's efforts to extend KCP-like reforms to other sites have been placed on hold or are being revised, and NNSA's plans on how to further implement KCP-like reforms are still being determined. DOE and NNSA reviews of the security breach indicated that its underlying causes may have been related to implementation of reforms similar to some of those implemented at KCP. For example, a 2012 review of the security breach by the DOE's Office of Inspector General noted that a breakdown in oversight, specifically one based on monitoring the contractor's systems instead of compliance with requirements, did not alert site officials to conditions that led to the breach.[29]

In the aftermath of the security breach, NNSA and DOE have moved cautiously to reevaluate or revise reforms, and agency officials told us it is

---

[27]NNSA, *Transformational Governance and Oversight*, NNSA Policy Letter, NAP-21 (Washington, D.C.: Feb. 28, 2011).

[28]We reported on the safety aspects of this reform effort in GAO, *Nuclear Safety: DOE Needs to Determine the Costs and Benefits of Its Safety Reform Effort* GAO-12-347 (Washington: D.C.: Apr. 20, 2012). We have work under way looking at NNSA's security reform efforts.

[29]U.S. Department of Energy, Office of Inspector General, Office of Audits and Inspections, *Special Report: Inquiry Into the Security Breach at the National Nuclear Security Administration's Y-12 National Security Complex*, DOE/IG-0868 (Washington, D.C.: Aug. 29, 2012).

still determining how reforms will be implemented in the future. NNSA is currently reevaluating how to implement some of the principal aspects of the KCP reforms identified earlier in this report—streamlining requirements, refocusing federal oversight, and establishing clear contractor goals, including:

- **Streamlining operating requirements.** Since the July 2012 Y-12 security breach, NNSA has been reassessing the need for some NNSA-specific policies. For example, NNSA initiated actions to rescind certain NNSA security policies and reinstate DOE's security directives. NNSA initiated these actions in response to a recommendation made in 2012 by the NNSA Security Task Force—a task force established by the NNSA Administrator in August 2012 to assess NNSA's security organization and oversight in the wake of the Y-12 security breach. As of March 2014, according to NNSA officials, NNSA sites were in varying stages of incorporating the DOE directives into their contracts and implementing the associated requirements.

- **Refocusing federal oversight.** Since the July 2012 Y-12 security breach, NNSA has been reviewing the use of contractor assurance systems in its oversight model and for evaluating contractor performance. According to a February 2013 report by the Office of Inspector General, the July 2012 Y-12 security breach highlighted the negative outcomes that may result when contractor assurance systems are too heavily relied on for federal oversight.[30] The February 2013 report noted that the Y-12 contractor's assurance system did not identify or correct major security problems that led to the security breach, and that while federal oversight staff knew of some security problems, they believed that the agency's oversight approach of relying on the contractor assurance system prevented them from intervening in contractor activities to correct problems. In reevaluating NNSA's oversight approaches, according to the Associate Principal Deputy Administrator, the agency is continuing to work on establishing contractor assurance systems but is moving toward using these systems to enable, rather than replace, federal oversight. In addition, according to the official, NNSA has recommitted to strengthening oversight, both by working to ensure sufficient oversight staff are in

---

[30]U.S. Department of Energy, Office of Inspector General, Office of Audits and Inspections, *National Nuclear Security Administration Contractor Governance*, DOE/IG-0881 (Washington, D.C.: Feb. 19, 2013).

place in field offices and by leveraging independent oversight by DOE's HSS.[31] According to NNSA's Acting Assistant Administrator for Infrastructure and Operations, as of February 2014, the agency was looking at opportunities to evaluate how best to use contractor assurance systems and data in federal oversight of contractor performance and was currently revising its oversight policy.[32]

- **Setting clear contractor goals** and meaningful incentives. Prior to the July 2012 Y-12 security breach, NNSA had been reassessing how it evaluated contractor performance and held contractors responsible for meeting agency goals. In fiscal year 2013, NNSA introduced its Strategic Performance Evaluation Plan, which lays out broad, common goals to which each site must contribute to achieve the overall agency mission. According an NNSA headquarters official, the plan streamlines NNSA evaluation of contractor performance by focusing on each site's contribution to the common set of desired agency outcomes—such as its nuclear weapons mission, and science and technology objectives. The official indicated that NNSA will evaluate each site using a standardized set of ratings as defined in regulation to replace the previous system of unique site-office-developed and site-office-evaluated performance ratings. According to the NNSA official, the Strategic Performance Evaluation Plan should help ensure consistent performance evaluation across the enterprise.[33]

Although some opportunities may exist for implementing KCP-like reforms at other NNSA sites, since the Y-12 security breach, NNSA officials and studies we reviewed noted that key factors enabling implementation of the reforms at KCP may not be present across the nuclear security enterprise. As noted above, these factors include having (1) high-level support for such reforms at NNSA headquarters; (2) specific site conditions to enable implementation, such as having a contractor with a single parent corporation and work activities that are solely nonnuclear in nature; and (3) a cooperative federal-contractor relationship. First, regarding high-level headquarters support for extending the KCP reforms,

---

[31] Under a recent departmental reorganization, this office is now called the Office of Independent Enterprise Assessments.

[32] We currently have work under way looking at this issue.

[33] According to a KCP Field Office official, the new plan may adversely affect the ability of field offices to focus performance goals on meeting site-specific mission objectives, as was the case at KCP.

NNSA's Acting Assistant Administrator for Infrastructure and Operations told us, in February 2014, that critical organizational issues, such as clarifying headquarters' organization and establishing field office roles and responsibilities for overseeing contractors, were still being discussed within NNSA and need to be settled before moving forward on KCP-like reforms.

Second, most NNSA sites differ considerably from KCP (see table 1).

Table 1: Comparison of Site Conditions at the Kansas City Plant (KCP) and Other National Nuclear Security Administration (NNSA) Sites

NNSA site	Contractor	Member companies of limited liability company or corporate parent	Special nuclear material category	Hazard (cat. I, II, and III) nuclear facilities	High- explosives operations
KCP	Honeywell Federal Manufacturing & Technologies, LLC	1 corporate parent	Category IV	0	No
Y12 National Security Complex	Consolidated Nuclear Security, LLC[b]	4 member companies	Category I	33	No
Pantex Plant	Consolidated Nuclear Security, LLC[b]	4 member companies	Category I	18	Yes
Los Alamos National Laboratory	Los Alamos National Security, LLC	3 member companies; 1 member university	Category I	13	Yes
Lawrence Livermore National Laboratory	Lawrence Livermore National Security, LLC	4 member companies, 2 member universities	Category III	8	Yes
Sandia Laboratories[a]	Sandia Corporation	1 corporate parent	Category III	5	Yes
Nevada National Nuclear Security Site	National Security Technologies, LLC	5 member companies	Category I	4	Yes
Savannah River Site—Tritium Facilities	Savannah River Nuclear Solutions, LLC.	3 member companies	Category IV	9	No

Source: GAO analysis of NNSA data. | GAO-14-588

[a]Sandia National Laboratories consists of four sites—a main site in Albuquerque, NM, and smaller sites in California, Hawaii, and Nevada.

[b]In January 2013, NNSA awarded Consolidated Nuclear Security, LLC, a $22.8 billion contract to manage both the Pantex and Y12 sites. Due to bid protests, which have been resolved, the contractor will take over management of the site in July 2014.

For example, reports we reviewed noted that, because most NNSA sites are managed and operated by limited-liability companies made up of multiple member companies, instead of by a single parent corporation, adopting the reforms elsewhere would be challenging. According to the January 2008 study commissioned by the KCP to assess cost reductions from implementing the reforms, having multiple corporate partners could limit successful implementation of KCP-like reforms at other NNSA sites. Specifically, the study notes that a single corporate parent can more easily use existing corporate systems to oversee and manage its subsidiary M&O entity, whereas this model may not work with an M&O having multiple member organizations. In addition, as noted above, the KCP M&O contractor's parent company was a Fortune 100 company with, according to a KCP Field Office official, a strong commitment to quality. In addition, an April 2008 KCP Field Office review of the reforms noted that implementation was enabled at KCP because the site activities were considered low-risk and nonnuclear. The review stated that it was not clear how to apply similar reforms to other NNSA sites, most of which have some nuclear operations, nuclear or other high-risk materials, or nuclear waste requiring disposition. Further, the March 2008 review by the department's HSS noted that KCP is a unique operation within NNSA and that careful analysis would need to be done if consideration will be given to applying the reforms to other sites, particularly where hazards are more complex or where the contractor's ability to self-identify and correct program weaknesses is not mature.

Third, the January 2008 cost reductions study noted that having a single parent company governing the KCP M&O contractor for decades resulted in establishing a cooperative relationship between the federal government and its contractor. More specifically the study noted that successful implementation of reforms at KCP resulted, in part, from the mutual trust built between the field office and contractor staff. However, a February 2012 National Research Council report that examined NNSA's management of its three national security laboratories[34] found there had been an erosion of trust between NNSA and its laboratories, and it recommended the agency work toward rebuilding positive relationships

---

[34]National Research Council, *Managing for High Quality Science and Engineering at the NNSA National Security Laboratories*, under Department of Energy Contract No. DE-DT0001744, TO#7 (Washington, D.C.: Feb. 15, 2012). The three NNSA national security laboratories are Los Alamos National Laboratory, Sandia National Laboratories, and Lawrence Livermore National Laboratory.

with its laboratories. Diminished trust between NNSA and its sites was also highlighted in a recently issued report by a congressional advisory panel, which described the relationship as "dysfunctional."[35]

During the course of our work, in December 2013, the National Defense Authorization Act for Fiscal Year 2014 was enacted.[36] Section 3130 of the act required the NNSA Administrator to develop a feasibility study and plan for implementing the principles of the KCP pilot to additional facilities in the national security enterprise by June 2014. We agree that further study of the applicability, costs, and benefits of the KCP reforms is warranted, and, in light of the congressional direction to NNSA, we are not making recommendations at this time.

Agency Comments

We provided a draft of this report to NNSA for its review and comment. In written comments, reproduced in appendix I, NNSA generally concurred with the overall findings of the report. The agency noted that it continues to study the appropriateness of further expansion of the Kansas City Pilot oversight reforms to other sites and implementation of NNSA's governance policy. NNSA also provided technical comments that we incorporated, as appropriate.

We are sending copies of this report to the appropriate congressional committees, the Secretary of Energy, and other interested parties. In addition, the report is available at no charge on the GAO website at http://www.gao.gov.

---

[35]Congressional Advisory Panel on the Governance of the Nuclear Security Enterprise, Interim Report, (Washington, D.C.: April 2014). The panel's full report is expected in July 2014.

[36]Pub. L. No. 113-66, 127 Stat. 672.

GAO-14-588 Extension of Kansas City Reforms

If you or your staff members have any questions about this report, please contact me at (202) 512-3841 or trimbled@gao.gov. Contact points for our Offices of Congressional Relations and Public Affairs may be found on the last page of this report. GAO staff who made key contributions to this report are listed in appendix II.

David C. Trimble
Director, Natural Resources and Environment

Appendix I: Comments from the Department of Energy

 **Department of Energy**
Under Secretary for Nuclear Security
Administrator, National Nuclear Security Administration
Washington, DC 20585

July 3, 2014

Mr. David Trimble
Director
Natural Resources and Environment
Government Accountability Office
Washington, DC 20458

Dear Mr. Trimble:

Thank you for the opportunity to review the Government Accountability Office's (GAO) draft report titled, *"National Nuclear Security Administration (NNSA) Expanded Use of Some Federal Oversight Reforms, but Future Plans Are Uncertain."* The GAO began this review in response to a mandate from the fiscal year 2012 National Defense Authorization Act to: 1) identify key reforms implemented at the Kansas City Plant (KCP) and reported benefits; 2) describe the key factors that NNSA, KCP and others identified as helping the site implement reforms; and 3) provide information on how NNSA has implemented or plans to implement similar reforms at other sites.

NNSA appreciates the auditors' interaction during the audit and GAO's efforts in highlighting the significant reforms at KCP including: a) streamlining operating requirements by adopting industry standards for lower risk activities, b) refocusing federal oversight to rely on contractor performance data, and c) establishing clear contractor goals and incentives. An independent audit verified a $14 million cost reduction related to these reforms for the KCP in 2008. Also, as noted in the report, NNSA has extended some elements of the reforms to other sites where appropriate. GAO notes that NNSA and DOE are re-evaluating some of these reforms after a July 2012 security breach at an NNSA site where overreliance on contractor self-assessments was identified by reviews as a contributing factor.

NNSA concurs with the overall audit facts and, with careful consideration of the causal factors leading to the Y-12 security breach, NNSA is continuing to study the appropriateness of further expansion of the Kansas City Pilot oversight reforms to other sites and implementation of NNSA's governance policy, NAP-21. NNSA has provided technical comments for GAO's consideration under separate cover to help improve the clarity and accuracy of the report.

2

If you have any questions regarding this response, please contact Dean Childs, Director, Office of Audit Coordination and Internal Affairs, at (301) 903-1341.

Sincerely,

Frank G. Klotz

Appendix II: GAO Contact and Staff Acknowledgments

GAO Contact	David C. Trimble, (202) 512-3841 or trimbled@gao.gov
Staff Acknowledgments	In addition to the individual named above, Jonathan Gill, Assistant Director; Nancy Kintner-Meyer; Cynthia Norris; and Kiki Theodoropoulos made key contributions to this report.

GAO's Mission	The Government Accountability Office, the audit, evaluation, and investigative arm of Congress, exists to support Congress in meeting its constitutional responsibilities and to help improve the performance and accountability of the federal government for the American people. GAO examines the use of public funds; evaluates federal programs and policies; and provides analyses, recommendations, and other assistance to help Congress make informed oversight, policy, and funding decisions. GAO's commitment to good government is reflected in its core values of accountability, integrity, and reliability.
Obtaining Copies of GAO Reports and Testimony	The fastest and easiest way to obtain copies of GAO documents at no cost is through GAO's website (http://www.gao.gov). Each weekday afternoon, GAO posts on its website newly released reports, testimony, and correspondence. To have GAO e-mail you a list of newly posted products, go to http://www.gao.gov and select "E-mail Updates."
Order by Phone	The price of each GAO publication reflects GAO's actual cost of production and distribution and depends on the number of pages in the publication and whether the publication is printed in color or black and white. Pricing and ordering information is posted on GAO's website, http://www.gao.gov/ordering.htm. Place orders by calling (202) 512-6000, toll free (866) 801-7077, or TDD (202) 512-2537. Orders may be paid for using American Express, Discover Card, MasterCard, Visa, check, or money order. Call for additional information.
Connect with GAO	Connect with GAO on Facebook, Flickr, Twitter, and YouTube. Subscribe to our RSS Feeds or E-mail Updates. Listen to our Podcasts. Visit GAO on the web at www.gao.gov.
To Report Fraud, Waste, and Abuse in Federal Programs	Contact: Website: http://www.gao.gov/fraudnet/fraudnet.htm E-mail: fraudnet@gao.gov Automated answering system: (800) 424-5454 or (202) 512-7470
Congressional Relations	Katherine Siggerud, Managing Director, siggerudk@gao.gov, (202) 512-4400, U.S. Government Accountability Office, 441 G Street NW, Room 7125, Washington, DC 20548
Public Affairs	Chuck Young, Managing Director, youngc1@gao.gov, (202) 512-4800 U.S. Government Accountability Office, 441 G Street NW, Room 7149 Washington, DC 20548

Please Print on Recycled Paper.